QUILTS *for*
Ice Cream Lovers

Janet Jones Worley

American Quilter's Society

P. O. Box 3290 • Paducah, KY 42002-3290
FAX 270-898-1173 *www.americanquilter.com*

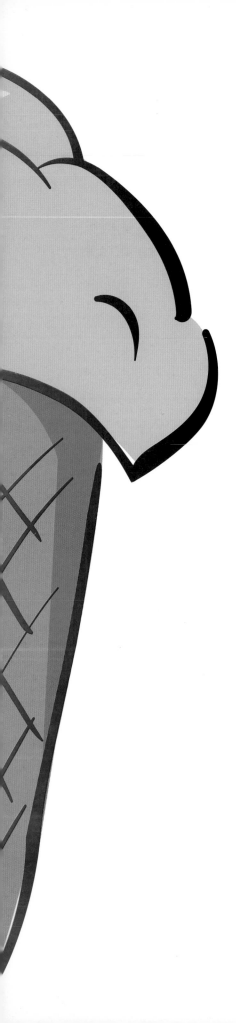

Located in Paducah, Kentucky, the American Quilter's Society (AQS) is dedicated to promoting the accomplishments of today's quilters. Through its publications and events, AQS strives to honor today's quiltmakers and their work and to inspire future creativity and innovation in quiltmaking.

Editor: Linda Baxter Lasco
Graphic Design: Amy Chase
Cover Design: Michael Buckingham
Photography: Charles R. Lynch

Library of Congress Cataloging-in-Publication Data
Worley, Janet Jones.
  Quilts for ice cream lovers / by Janet Jones Worley.
    p. cm.
Summary: "Author provides clear and thorough instructions with step-by-step directions and diagrams for making large and small quilts. Piecing and some appliqué embellishment. For all skill levels"-- Provided by publisher.
  ISBN 978-1-57432-925-4
1. Quilting--Patterns. 2. Patchwork--Patterns. 3. Appliqué--Patterns.
4. Ice cream, ices, etc.   I. Title.

TT835.W682 2007
746.46'041--dc22
                    2006100738

Additional copies of this book may be ordered from the American Quilter's Society, PO Box 3290, Paducah, KY 42002-3290; 800-626-5420 (orders only please); or online at www.AmericanQuilter.com. For all other inquiries, please call 270-898-7903.

Dedication

To my husband, Michael, who has always been my greatest supporter, and to my grandmother, Sadie Schwetman, and Michael's grandmother, Beulah Knowles, two ladies I love and miss every day.

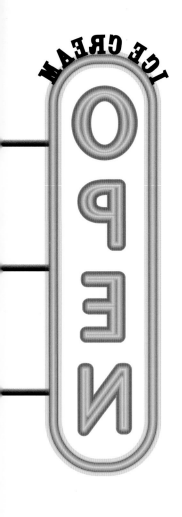

Acknowledgments

Writing a second book would not have been possible without the love and support of so many people. Thank you! Remember, you're my favorites!

My gratitude to ...

• The wonderful manufacturers and people listed in the Resources section.

• Bernina® of America, Inc., and the Bernina Stitch Regulator, which I used on every quilt.

• Beth Hayes, friend and editor extraordinaire—an amazing woman who started me on the path.

• My wonderful friends Kim (Kimma) Martin Battles, Mary Wood, Diana Hofmann, Pam LaPier, and my nephew, Michael and Brent Locke, and Michael's wife, Ann, who all love ice cream; also to Debbie Bowles, owner of Maple Island Quilts; also Kelly and Kim Corbridge for making the most wonderful cutting table, and to Kelly for giving it to me!

• Bunny, my standard poodle, who personally owns five quilts and tests each quilt as the binding is being done.

• My students, who have inspired me more than they will ever know.

• Bonnie Browning for her encouragement.

• Linda Baxter Lasco, my wonderful editor.

Contents

Introduction

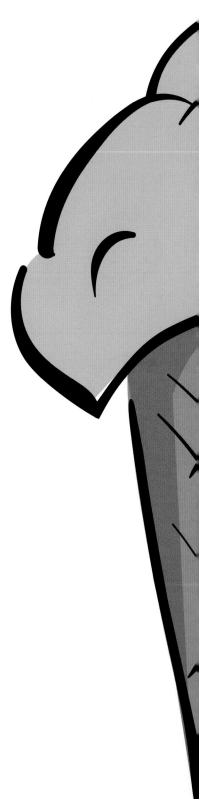

This all started with chocolate and my *Quilts for Chocolate Lovers* book. Now my inspiration is ice cream. While you may not find ice cream in every quilt class, it is a good bet you will find many quilters treating themselves to some at lunch or when class is over. Let your imagination fly next time you enter an ice cream parlor and you will be amazed at the quilts ice cream will inspire.

Like all quilters, I wish I had more time to actually quilt. We all live such busy lives that finding time for the things we really want to do takes some planning. I must admit I love the instant gratification of a quick quilt project, but I want it to be wonderful, too. I have included many small projects in this book with all of that in mind. My personal favorite is the Snip and Toss Cone Caddy—first, because it is fun and easy to make and second, because it makes a great gift. In class, it's a hoot to see what everyone comes up with. Be sure to give this one a try.

I have noticed that many quilters work so hard on their projects, they're almost making quilting into a job. Quilting is what we do for fun! Relax and enjoy the process. The more you quilt the better you will become. If you are short on time, just quilt for twenty minutes or so. Any amount of time is better than none.

In my opinion, perfection is overrated. The next time someone looks at one of your quilts and says, "How beautiful!" you only need to say three small words: "Why, thank you," and nothing else. Don't sigh about the points that are hiding or squares that are not perfectly square. Just accept the compliment and move on to your next project.

My Approach

Preparation

Before beginning any quilting project, make sure your rotary blade is sharp and your sewing machine needle is new. Brush all the lint out of your machine and bobbin case before starting.

Fabric

Use 100 percent cotton in all the quilt projects shown. If you have trouble choosing fabrics for your projects, try letting the fabric collections do the work for you. No more pulling your hair out trying to decide if this color goes with that. If it is in the collection, it will work. To me, the most important question in fabric selection is, "Do I like it?" Your quilt must please you.

Select a fabric you really love and then build your other fabric choices around it. The paisley print in CHOCOLATE RIPPLE was the one used to pick out all the other fabrics in that quilt (see page 48). The large print in GIRLIE GIRL GRAPE is another fabric that determined the choice of all the other fabrics in the quilt (see page 52).

If you do not prewash your fabrics, you are taking a chance that one of them will bleed into your other fabrics. I must admit that I live on the wild side. No prewashing for me. Someday this will come back to bite me, but until that day comes, like Scarlett O'Hara, "I'll worry about that tomorrow."

The best tool you can have in your studio is a digital camera. Use it to "interview" fabrics. Quilts can really change once the center is finished. Pin your tops to a design wall with different border fabrics. It is amazing what the camera can see that the eye can miss.

Appliqué

For appliqué, use the method of your choice. I like using paper-backed fusible web. Each brand of fusible web comes with its own manufacturer's instructions. Every brand needs to be handled in a slightly different way for it to work properly.

Secure the threads at the beginning and ending of your appliqué stitching line. With the buttonhole stitch, hand securing the threads gives the best results. To finish by machine, turn the stitch width to zero and the stitch length almost as low as it will go. Make six or seven of these tiny stitches as close as possible to your appliqué piece. Using a polyester monofilament thread in the bobbin creates a much smoother stitch.

The Scoop on Fusing: Trace the appliqué template onto the paper side of fusible web and cut out leaving ⅛" to ¼" around the drawn line. Following manufacturer's directions, fuse the web to the wrong side of the fabric and cut out on the drawn line. Don't remove the paper until you're ready to fuse the pieces onto the background fabric.

Begin with a pair of squares.

Half-Square Triangles

Yardage for making half-square triangles is based on the method of using two squares of fabric to make the half-square triangle units. Draw a diagonal line on the wrong side of the lighter of the two fabrics, place them right sides together, stitch two lines ¼" on both sides of the drawn line, and cut the units apart on the drawn line. Press the seam allowances toward the darker fabric.

Layer squares right sides together.

Mark a diagonal line through the center of the top square.

Sew diagonal seam lines ¼" from the center drawn line.

Cut the squares in half along the drawn line.

Corner-Square Flying Geese Units

Yardage for making Flying Geese units is based on the corner-square method of using two squares of one fabric and a rectangle of a contrasting fabric.

Each pair of squares yields 2 half-square triangles.

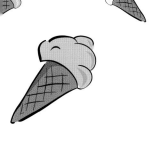

- Draw a diagonal line on the back of the two squares.

- Align one square with the end of the rectangle, right sides together, with the diagonal line as shown.

- Sew along the diagonal line, trim the seam allowance to ¼", and press.

- Align the other square with the other end of the rectangle, right sides together.

- Sew along the diagonal line, trim the seam allowance to ¼", and press.

To make a half-Flying Geese unit, sew one square to one end of a rectangle. Sew along the diagonal line, trim the seam allowance to ¼", and press.

Use two 2½" squares and a 2½" x 4½" rectangle.

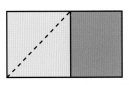
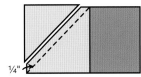

Mark and sew a diagonal line.   Trim the corner.

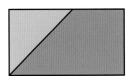
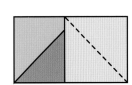

Press open.   Mark and sew diagonally.

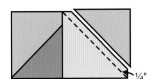
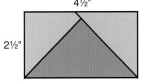

Trim the corner.   Press open. Block is the same size as the original rectangle.

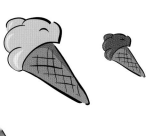

Setting Triangles

Exact measurements for side and corner setting triangles are given in the cutting instructions. However, I never cut my own triangles the accurate size. I always add a least 1" or 2" and do my piecing with the larger triangles. Then I'll square the blocks before joining them together and square the top before adding borders. You'll be amazed at how this simple trick can square your quilts and make them hang straight.

Borders

Square up your quilt top before adding borders. Measure the length from top to bottom through the center of the quilt top, not along the sides, to determine the correct measurement for the side borders.

Piece the border fabric strips as necessary and cut the side borders to length. After the borders are sewn and the seam allowance is pressed toward the border, measure the width through the center of the quilt top, including the side borders, to determine the correct measurement for the top and bottom borders. Piece as required, cut, stitch, and press.

Quilting

Pin baste for machine quilting using #1 quilting safety pins. Try to keep from placing pins in the quilting line area to make life easier. As you quilt, just remove the pins as you come to them.

Stitch in the ditch with a walking foot and free-motion quilt with a darning foot, sometimes called a free-motion foot, embroidery foot, or quilting foot. Start in the middle of the quilt and work out toward the edges. Lowering the feed dogs will allow you to stitch in any direction without ever turning your quilt. Remember to blink, breathe, and have fun. Free-motion quilting will set you free!

Whenever possible, I stitch in the ditch on all quilts. It makes the quilt lie flat and smooth. If the fabric is busy, heavy or pattern quilting will be lost.

Binding

To be honest I love every part of quilting but binding is my favorite! This is the time I can admire my quilt as I hand sew down the binding. The most popular binding is double-fold French binding. Cut the binding strips 2½" wide across the fabric from selvage to selvage. Cut enough strips to go around the entire quilt. Sew the strips together end to end with diagonal seams. Press the long strip in half lengthwise, wrong sides together. Place the binding on the quilt top, aligning the raw edges of the binding with the raw edges of the quilt and stitch with your walking foot.

If I'm running short of fabric, I sometimes cut my binding 1⅜" and apply it without a double fold. I find it easier to miter the corners with this method because there is less bulk. The single thickness does not wear as well, but I don't find that's a problem with wallhangings.

Embellishing with Beads

Put some sparkle into your quilt with beads, yarns, threads, buttons, or whatever else comes your way. Let your imagination soar!

Many years ago I was teaching at a wonderful guild in Texas. After class, a few ladies asked if I'd mind stopping by a bead shop on the way back to the hotel. Of course I didn't mind and was happy to go, thinking to myself that it wasn't a place I'd spend any money. Ha! Later that evening, much poorer but with a bag full of beads, I was hooked. Now, each time I find a fabric I love, I also shop for beads.

Machine Beading

I often teach machine beading in my classes, and many of my students are surprised that it can be done so easily. With just a few supplies, you can put beads on your quilts that will stay on. I haven't lost a bead yet.

I like to purchase beads from a shop specializing in beads because they will sell beads individually. If you are unsure about your needle fitting through a bead, take a needle with you when you

shop and try it out. This is much better than breaking a needle or a bead. All the beads stitched on FAT QUARTER SUNDAE (except for the fringe) were done by machine (see page 20). Stitching through fusible web is difficult by hand but fast and easy by machine.

Supplies

- Plastic hoop with a metal inner ring that springs open to hold the fabric or quilt
- Clear polyester monofilament thread, also known as invisible thread
- 60/8 machine needle
- Straight stitch throat plate (optional)

Once you are accustomed to machine beading, you will be putting beads on very quickly, but it is best to start out slowly. First, drop the feed dogs on your machine. All beading is done free-motion. Remove the foot from machine, put on the straight stitch throat plate, and thread the machine with clear polyester thread in both the bobbin and top. It is important that you use this thread because a bead can take on the color of the thread securing it. Clear thread keeps the color crisp and clear.

Hoop the fabric and secure your threads right where the first bead will be placed. Bring the bobbin thread to the top of the fabric. Gently but firmly, hold both top and bobbin threads and take at least three very tiny stitches.

With needle in the up position, place a bead on the needle up to the eye of needle and no farther. Gently keep a finger against the bead to hold it in place and turn the fly wheel to bring the needle down to the fabric. Release the bead and complete the stitch, with the needle ending in the up position.

Barely move the quilt (and I am serious about barely) until the needle is pointing outside the bead. Now take another stitch. Keeping the threads taut will make your bead sit up. This is the way all your beads should look. Every once in a while a bead will not sit up on its own and you will have to move it with your

Quilts for Ice Cream Lovers ∴ Janet Jones Worley

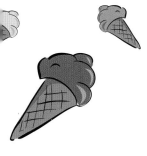

finger. Take a couple of very tiny stitches to secure your threads. That's all there is to it.

Because my quilts are handled on a daily basis, I take about five stitches in and out of a bead to make sure it stays in place. If you do this, be sure you always come out to the side of the bead at the same spot.

 *The Scoop:* Use the hand wheel until you are comfortable putting beads on by machine. Once you are comfortable you will no longer need to use it and can take stitches quickly.

Beading by Hand

I prefer to use a hand-appliqué needle to do my hand beading. The very long thin beading needles do not work as well for beading on quilts. Beading thread Nymo D is a very common thread that can be purchased just about anywhere and is stronger than regular cotton thread. You will see this thread on paper bobbins and in many colors. I secure my threads using the everyday quilter's knot, which is made by wrapping the end of the thread around the needle about 3 or 4 times and pulling the needle through the wraps until the knot is at the end of thread.

To add a single bead, use the knotted thread and bring the needle up from wrong side of the quilt. String a bead onto the thread and go back through the quilt, then back up through the bead again. Secure your threads right beside the bead.

For another great beading look, knot the thread and bring it up from the wrong side of the quilt right through the hole of a single bead. To secure this bead to the quilt, add another smaller bead to the thread and stitch back through the larger bead to the wrong side. This places the smaller bead on top of the larger one and adds a great dimensional look to your project. This is the method I used to put beads on the RED VELVET ICE CREAM quilt (page 66).

The back stitch is what I use most often when putting on more than one bead by hand. Come up from the wrong side of the quilt and add three beads to your thread, then bring the needle through to the back. Bring the needle back up through the quilt near the second bead. Run the needle through the second and third bead, pull taunt, and sew through the third bead. After you have exited the third bead you can again add three beads and repeat as often as you like. You can add five beads at a time if you're using 15/0s or smaller beads.

Beading Fringe

Adding bead fringe to the bottom of a wall quilt is a fun, easy way to add sparkle to your project. First, finish the binding on your quilt. Then knot a strand of beading thread and bring the needle down through the binding and out the bottom of the binding. Add a variety of beads to the thread. Finally, go through a sequin or larger bead and back through all the strung beads and the binding. End with a few stitches in the back of the binding.

Remember, beads do not have to be round. I used triangular, square, and rectangular beads on my FAT QUARTER SUNDAE quilt (page 20). I strung different numbers of beads on each strand so they would hang at different levels. I also used sequins in various shades to hang from the bottom of the fringe for a bright, fun look. Use anything you desire in place of the sequins, such as teardrop beads, large round beads, or even charms. I placed my strands approximately one-eighth inch apart.

Quilt size: 49" x 49"
Finished block size: 8½" x 8½"

FOUR SCOOPS, PLEASE, made by the author

This quilt has three-dimensional pinwheels (the "scoops") to make you sit up and take notice. The soft colors and bright greens remind me of the wonderful afternoons I spent with my grandmother having ice cream on her porch.

If you prefer, you can use fat quarters for the scoop and triangle prints rather than yardage cut off the bolt.

Yardage and Cutting

Use fabric at least 40" wide. Cut strips selvage to selvage.

Fabric	Yards	First Cut	Second Cut
5 prints for the scoops	¼ each	See the Scoop & Triangle Cutting table	
5 prints for the triangles	¼ each	See the Scoop & Triangle Cutting table	
White background	1 ½	5 strips 3 ½"	52 A □ 3 ½" x 3 ½"
		2 strips 5 ⅛"	8 ◩ 5 ⅛" x 5 ⅛"(16 B triangles)
		1 strip 6 ⅞"	2 ◩ 6 ⅞" x 6 ⅞"(4 C triangles)
		1 strip 13 ¼"	2 ⊠ 13 ¼" x 13 ¼" (8 D triangles)
Inner border stripe	½	5 strips 2 ½"	
Inner border prairie points	⅝	5 strips 3 ½"	52 A □ 3 ½" x 3 ½"
Outer border	⅞	5 strips 5"	
Backing	3 ⅜	2 panels 40" x 57"	
Binding	⅝	6 strips 2 ½"	
Batting		57" x 57"	

Scoop & Triangle Cutting

	Scoop prints		Triangle prints	
	First Cut	Second Cut	First Cut	Second Cut
	No. of strips	No. of A squares	No. of strips	No. of B squares
	3 ½"	3 ½" x 3 ½"	5 ⅛"	5 ⅛" x 5 ⅛" cut in half diagonally
Red	2	20	1	6
Green	2	12	1	4
Yellow	2	12	1	4
Blue	1	4	1	2
Pink	1	4	1	2

Block Construction

1. Fold the scoop print A squares in half diagonally twice (fig. 1). Press.

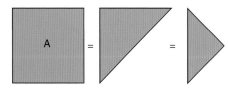

Fig. 1. Folding the "scoops"

2. Place a scoop on an A background square, aligning the raw edges. Make sure the open fold is on the left (fig. 2). Use a

water-soluble glue stick to hold the scoop in place. Repeat to make four scoop units.

Fig. 2. Aligning the raw edges

3. Arrange the four scoop units in a pinwheel (fig. 3) and join them with ¼" seam allowances to form the center of the block.

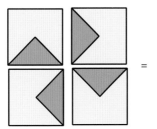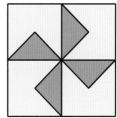

Fig. 3. Assembling the center pinwheel

4. Add the B triangles to complete the block (fig. 4).

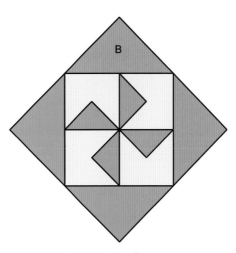

Fig. 4. Adding B triangles

5. Referring to the Scoop and Triangle Cutting table, make 13 blocks.

Quilt Assembly

1. Join the blocks and the white C and D setting triangles in diagonal rows (fig. 5, page 18).

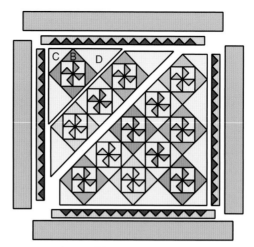

2. Determine the measurement for the side inner borders. Cut two 2½" inner border strips to that length.

3. To make the prairie points, fold the 52 A squares in half twice diagonally, just as you did for the scoops. Press.

Fig. 5. Quilt assembly

4. Lay 13 prairie points along a side inner border strip, starting and ending ¼" in from the ends and making sure the open folds all point to the left.

5. Open the folded side and slip in the next prairie point, adjusting the spacing until all 13 fit evenly (fig. 6). Pin them in place. Sew with a scant ¼" seam allowance. Repeat for the other side of the quilt.

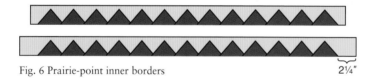

Fig. 6 Prairie-point inner borders   2¼"

6. In the same way, cut the top and bottom inner border strips and add 13 prairie points to each, starting and ending 2¼" in from the ends. Sew to the quilt.

7. Measure, cut, and sew the outer border strips to the sides of the quilt top.

8. For the top and bottom outer borders, you will need to join half of a 5" strip to each of the remaining two 5" strips. Measure, cut, and sew the outer border strips to the top and bottom of the quilt.

Finishing

Layer the quilt top, batting, and backing; baste. Quilt the layers together then bind the raw edges to complete your quilt.

Seven Days Celebration

Long ago I decided to take a full week to celebrate my birthday. It took a few years to bring my husband around, but now he plans it all himself. Why limit yourself to a single day?

The three quilts that follow, FAT QUARTER SUNDAE, PARTY HATS, AND IS THAT FOR ME? are great quilts to make for anyone having a special occasion to celebrate. They are all perfect to make with a child. Start a new family tradition. Bring out these special quilts to decorate a wall or table when a friend or family member has something to celebrate.

As for me, I love birthday week. And what is a birthday week or any celebration without ice cream?

Fat Quarter Sundae

Quilt size: 15½" x 17¾"

FAT QUARTER SUNDAE, made by the author

The success of this small quilt depends on your doing some research. I have only provided a template for a single ice cream scoop. But each scoop of ice cream melts differently. This is where the research comes in. You have to see what other scoops look like as they melt so you can accurately depict the drips. Ah, the hard life of a quilter!

Yardage and Cutting

Use fabric at least 40" wide. Cut strips selvage to selvage.

Fabric	Yards	Cut
Assorted white		
with black prints	2 fat quarters	1 ☐ 9" x 9" (sundae background)
		1 ▭ 5" x 9" (cone background)
		1 ▭ 3 ½" x 14" (scoops background)
Assorted black		
with white prints	4 fat quarters	2 strips 1" (sashing)
		1 strip 3" x 12 ½" (left side border)
		1 strip 1 ½" x 16 ½" (top border)
		1 strip 3" x 16 ½" (bottom border)
		1 strip 2 ¼" x 16" (right side border)
		1 ▭ 5" x 8" (bowl)
9 prints for the ice cream	scraps	9 ☐ 4" x 4"
Tan for ice cream cone	scrap 3" x 5"	1 ▭ 3" x 5"
Backing	1 panel	20" x 22"
Binding	¼ yd.	2 strips 2 ½"
Batting		20" x 22"

Additional Materials

¼ yard fusible web
¼ yard tear-away or water-soluble stabilizer
Bead fringe (optional)
Beads (optional)
Beading thread and appliqué needles (optional)

Block Construction

1. See The Scoop on Fusing on page 8. Trace, cut, and fuse the templates to the wrong side of the bowl, cone, and ice cream scoop fabrics. You need nine scoops with varying drip patterns.

2. Cut the shapes along the drawn lines. Do not remove the paper backing until you are ready to fuse the pieces in place.

3. Fold the three background pieces in quarters and finger press to establish placement lines. Remove the paper backing as you lay the

appliqué pieces on the right side of the appropriate backgrounds (fig. 1). When all the pieces have been arranged on a background piece, fuse them in place.

4. Place tear-away or water-soluble stabilizer under each unit and finish the fused edges with a zigzag or buttonhole stitch. Remove the stabilizer.

Quilt Assembly and Finishing

1. Join the appliqué units and sashing strips, then add the borders (fig. 1).

2. Layer the quilt top, batting, and backing; baste. Quilt the layers together then bind the raw edges to complete your quilt.

Fig. 1. Quilt assembly

Design suggestion: Add bead fringe to the bottom edge of your quilt and sew bead "sprinkles" on the scoops using beading thread and appliqué needles.

Quilting suggestion: Quilt a waffle pattern into the ice cream cone. Use beads to accent the pattern.

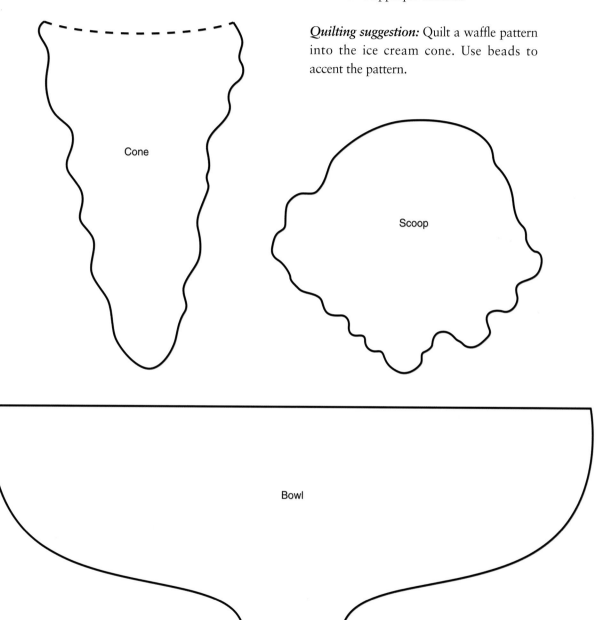

Cone

Scoop

Bowl

Party Hats

Quilt size: 32" x 40"
Finished block size: 9" x 13"

PARTY HATS, made by the author

Personalize these hats by choosing fabrics that reflect family members' special interests or hobbies. Go wild with embellishments—pompoms, pinwheels, bells, beads, ribbons, or fancy fibers.

Yardage and Cutting

Use fabric at least 40" wide. Cut strips selvage to selvage.

Fabric	Yards	First Cut	Second Cut
Party hats	4 fat quarters	4 ☐ 8 ½" x 11"	
Yellow background	½	1 strip 13 ½"	4 ☐ 9 ½" x 13 ½"
Blue sashing and inner border	½	6 strips 2 ½"	6 ☐ 2 ½" x 13 ½"
			3 ☐ 2 ½" x 24 ½"
Border	⅝	4 strips 4 ½"	4 strips 4 ½" x 32 ½"
Backing	1 ⅓	1 panel 36" x 44"	
Binding	⅜	4 strips 2 ½"	
Batting		36" x 44"	

Additional Materials

8½" x 11" sheet of paper
½ yard fusible web
½ yard tear-away or water-soluble stabilizer
Embellishments

Block Construction

1. To make the hat template, fold the 8½" x 11" sheet of paper in half lengthwise. Trim as shown in figure 1.

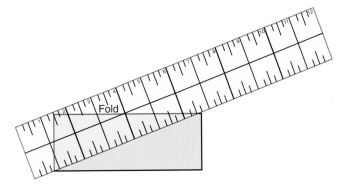

Fig. 1. Making the hat template

2. Use the template to cut four hats from the party hat fabrics.

3. See The Scoop on Fusing on page 8. Fuse a hat to the right

side of each of the four background rectangles, as shown in the assembly diagram (fig. 2).

4. Place tear-away or water-soluble stabilizer under each block and finish the fused edges with a zigzag or buttonhole stitch. Remove the stabilizer. Embellish the hats as desired.

Quilt Assembly

Assemble the blocks, sashing strips, and borders as shown in figure 2.

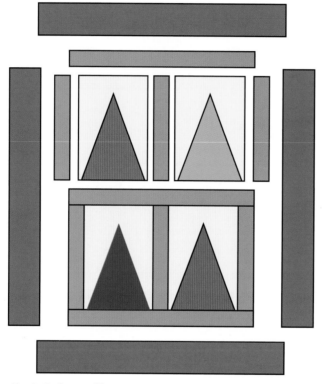

Fig. 2. Quilt assembly

Finishing

Layer the quilt top, batting, and backing; baste. Quilt the layers together then bind the raw edges to complete your quilt.

Quilting suggestion: Keep the quilting as simple as possible to make this quilt quick to finish. Using a walking foot, quilt in the ditch around all the hats, blocks, and inner borders. Stitch an additional line of quilting in the center of the inner border. Free-motion quilt the border with a medium-sized meander.

Is That for Me?

Quilt size: 34" x 40"
Finished block size: 6" x 8"

IS THAT FOR ME? made by the author

"Wrap" these presents with a mix of appliquéd or three-dimensional bows, or with trims, ribbon, rickrack, beads, or decorative stitches in fancy threads. The sky's the limit!

Yardage and Cutting

Use fabric at least 40" wide. Cut strips selvage to selvage.

Fabric	Yards	First Cut	Second Cut
Gifts .... scraps		9 ☐ 6 ½" x 8 ½"	
Appliqué bows .... scraps		3 ☐ 6" x 6"	
Ties for dimensional bows ... scraps		16 strips 1 ½" x 9 ½"	
Black.................................... 1 ⅛			
corner squares		1 strip 4 ½".........................	4 ☐ 4 ½" x 4 ½"
sashing & inner border		12 strips 2 ½".....................	6 strips 2 ½" x 8 ½"
			2 strips 2 ½" x 22 ½"
			2 strips 2 ½" x 26 ½"
			2 strips 2 ½" x 28 ½"
Outer border.......................... ⅝		4 strips 4 ½".....................	2 strips 4 ½" x 26 ½"
			2 strips 4 ½" x 32 ½"
Backing .... 1 ⅓		1 panel 38" x 44"	
Binding................................. ⅜		5 strips 2 ½"	
Batting..................................		38" x 44"	

Additional Materials

½ yard fusible web
½ yard tear-away or water-soluble stabilizer
1½" x 2½" piece of template plastic
Ribbon or rickrack

Block Construction

Appliqué Bows

1. See The Scoop on Fusing on page 8. Trace three sets of appliqué bows (templates A, B, B reverse, and C on page 30) on the paper side of the fusible web. Fuse the templates to the wrong side of each appliqué bow fabric and cut the pieces on the traced lines.

2. Fold three of the gift fabrics in quarters and finger press the creases to establish appliqué placement lines. Remove the paper from the bow pieces. Arrange them on the right side of the gift fabrics in alphabetical order (fig. 1). Fuse them in place.

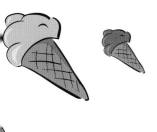

3. Place tear-away or water-soluble stabilizer under the bows and finish the fused edges with a zigzag or buttonhole stitch. Remove the stabilizer.

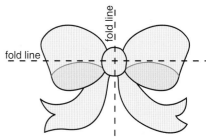

Fig. 1. Bow placement

Dimensional Bows

1. Trace the pattern for the Tied Bow End onto template plastic and cut the template. Use it to round off one end of each of the sixteen tie strips. Place two strips right sides together and sew the two long sides and the rounded end with a ¼" seam allowance. Clip the curve, turn the strips right side out, and press to complete one tie. Make eight ties.

2. Fold four of the gift fabrics in half as shown and finger press to establish a placement line across the middle. Sew the open ends of the ties ⅛" from the edges of the gift fabric as shown (fig. 2). Sew ties to four of the gift fabrics. Pin the ties together until the quilt is completed.

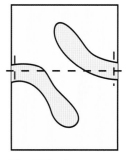

Fig. 2. Tie placement

Remaining Packages

Use ribbon or rickrack to "tie" the remaining two gift packages.

Quilt Assembly

Assemble the blocks, sashing strips, border strips and cornerstones as shown in figure 3.

Finishing

Layer the quilt top, batting, and backing; baste. Quilt the layers together. Embellish as desired. Bind the raw edges. Tie the three-dimensional bows to complete your quilt.

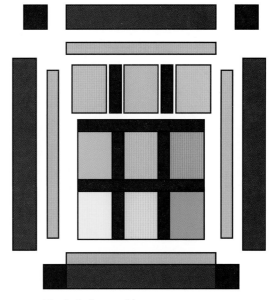

Fig. 3. Quilt assembly

C

Br

B

A

Tied Bow End
template

Quilting suggestion: Quilt in the appliqué bow details as indicated on the template. Try free-motion quilting the outline of a gift box in the cornerstones.

Summertime Sherbet

Quilt size: 38" x 54"
Finished block size: 8" x 8"

SUMMERTIME SHERBET, made by the author

A great size for a gift … not too small and, most important, not too large. To add some sparkle, I stitched beads to the quilting motif. It's almost impossible for me to make a quilt these days without beads.

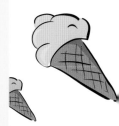

Yardage and Cutting

Use fabric at least 40" wide. Cut strips selvage to selvage.

Fabric	Yards	First Cut	Second Cut
Orange print	⅞	1 strip 2 ½"	8 A ▢ 2 ½" x 2 ½"
		5 strips 4 ½"	(outer border)
Orange tone-on-tone	¼	2 strips 2 ½"	32 B ▭ 2" x 2 ½"
Cream	1	2 strips 2 ½"	32 B ▭ 2" x 2 ½"
		3 strips 2 ⅜"	32 C ▢ 2 ⅜" x 2 ⅜"
		2 strips 8 ½"	7 E ▢ 8 ½" x 8 ½"
8 medium orange to gold prints	⅛ each	1 strip 3 ⅞" each fabric	2 ◨ 3 ⅞" x 3 ⅞" from each fabric (total 32 D triangles)
		trim 3 ⅞" strips to 2 ⅜"	2 C ▢ 2 ⅜" x 2 ⅜" from each fabric
		trim 2 ⅜" strips to 2 ½"	9 A ▢ 2 ½" x 2 ½" (total 72 A squares for pieced border)
Rust stripe		4 strips 1 ½"	(inner border)
Backing	1 ½	2 panels 23" x 62"	
Batting		46" x 62"	
Binding	⅝	6 strips 2 ½"	

Optional Materials
Beads for embellishment

Block Construction

1. As they are needed, cut the pieces listed in the yardage and cutting table.

2. Join 32 cream and 32 orange tone-on-tone B rectangles along their 2½" sides.

3. Sew rectangle units from step 2 to opposite sides of eight orange print A squares to make eight center-row units (fig. 1). You'll have 16 rectangle units remaining.

Fig. 1. Center-row unit

4. Following the Half-Square Triangle instructions on page 8, make 32 half-square triangle units with 16 medium-to-gold print C squares and 16 cream C squares.

Fig. 2. Corner-unit assembly

5. Cut 16 cream C squares in half diagonally. Sew two of the resulting triangles to each half-square-triangle unit as shown in figure 2. Add the orange-print D triangles to make 32 corner units.

6. Join the corner units, the remaining 16 rectangle units, and the eight center-row units to make eight blocks (fig. 3).

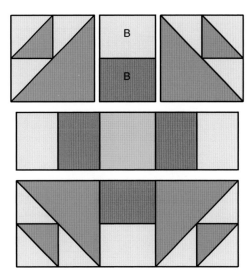

Fig. 3. Block assembly

Quilt Assembly

1. Assemble the quilt with five rows of three blocks, alternating the pieced blocks with the seven E squares (fig. 4).

2. Square up the quilt. Measure, cut, and apply the first inner border. Press the seam allowances toward the border. For the pieced border to fit, the quilt needs to measure 26½" x 42½" including the inner border and seam allowances.

3. Sew two rows of 21 A squares to make the side borders. Sew these to the sides of the quilt. Make two rows of 15 A squares and sew these to the top and bottom of the quilt. Press the seam allowances toward the inner border.

4. Measure, cut, and apply the outer borders. You will need to cut one 4½" border strip in half and sew each half to two other border strips for a piece long enough for the sides of the quilt.

Finishing

If you plan to machine bead your quilt top, do it before the quilt is basted.

Layer the quilt top, batting, and backing; baste. Quilt the layers together, then bind the raw edges to complete your quilt.

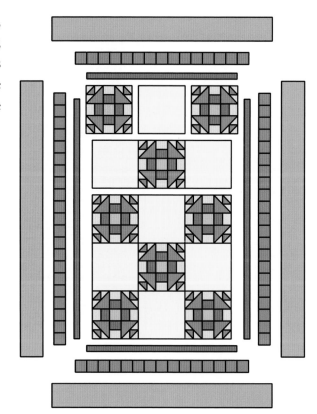

Fig. 4. Quilt assembly

Ice Cream Parlor

Quilt size: 46¾" x 46¾"
Finished block size: 11¼" x 11¼"

ICE CREAM PARLOR, made by the author

This is a fast-to-piece quilt that looks great in any fabric combination. I once taught on a quilting cruise to the Caribbean and had the time of my life. Every day, a booth by the pool would have free ice cream. The colors I chose for my quilt were the tropical colors I saw as I ate on my floating ice cream parlor.

Yardage and Cutting

Use fabric at least 40" wide. Cut strips selvage to selvage.

Fabric	Yards	First Cut	Second Cut
medium aqua	⅝	2 strips 3 ⅛"	20 A ☐ 3 ⅛" x 3 ⅛"
		2 strips 5 ⅜"	8 ◩ 5 ⅜" x 5 ⅜"
			(total 16 C triangles)
purple	½	1 strip 2 ¾"	5 B ☐ 2 ¾" x 2 ¾"
		3 strips 3 ⅛"	20 A ☐ 3 ⅛" x 3 ⅛"
			16 ◩ 3 ⅛" x 3 ⅛"
			(total 32 D triangles)
pink	⅜	3 strips 2 ¾"	36 B ☐ 2 ¾" x 2 ¾"
magenta	⅜	3 strips 2 ¾"	36 B ☐ 2 ¾" x 2 ¾"
dark pink	¼	2 strips 2 ¾"	24 B ☐ 2 ¾" x 2 ¾"
dark aqua	¼	2 strips 2 ¾"	20 B ☐ 2 ¾" x 2 ¾"
lavender	¼	2 strips 2 ¾"	16 B ☐ 2 ¾" x 2 ¾"
inner border	⅜	4 strips 2 ½"	
outer border	⅞	5 strips 5"	
backing	3 ⅜	2 panels 28" x 55"	
binding	⅝	6 strips 2 ½"	
batting		55" x 55"	

Block Construction

As they are needed, cut the pieces listed in the Yardage and Cutting table.

Block I

1. Following the Half-square-Triangle instructions on page 8, make 40 half-square triangle units with 20 each medium aqua and purple A squares (fig. 1).

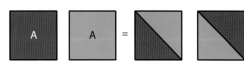

Fig. 1. Half-square triangle unit

2. Join two half-square-triangle units with two pink and magenta B squares to make 20 corner units (fig. 2).

3. Join the dark pink and dark aqua B squares to make 20 rectangle units (fig. 3).

4. Assemble block 1 with four corner units, four rectangle units, and one purple B square (fig. 4). Make five of block 1.

Block 2

1. Sew the purple D triangles to adjacent sides of the 16 remaining pink B squares and add the medium aqua C triangles to make 16 corner units (fig 5).

2. Make 16 rectangle units as in block 1 with lavender and magenta B squares.

3. Assemble block 2 with four corner units, four rectangle units, and one dark pink B square (fig. 6). Make four of block 2.

Quilt Assembly

1. Lay out the quilt top in three rows of three blocks, alternating the placement of block 1 and block 2 (fig. 7, page 38). Join the rows.

2. Square up the quilt top and, measuring through the center of the quilt as described in Borders on page 10, cut and apply the

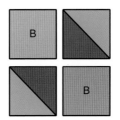

Fig. 2. Corner unit

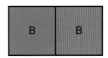

Fig. 3. Block-1 rectangle unit

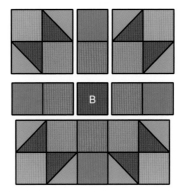

Fig. 4. Block-1 assembly

Fig. 5 Block-2 corner unit

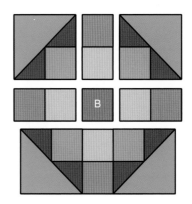

Fig. 6. Block-2 assembly

inner and outer borders. For the top and bottom outer border, you will need to join half of a 5" strip to two of the other 5" strips.

Finishing

Layer the quilt top, batting, and backing; baste. Quilt the layers together, then bind the raw edges to complete your quilt.

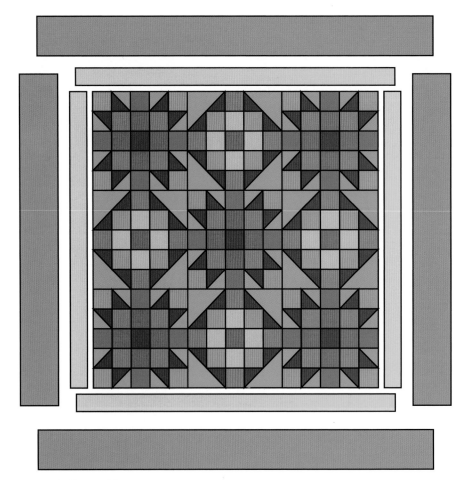

Fig. 7. Quilt assembly

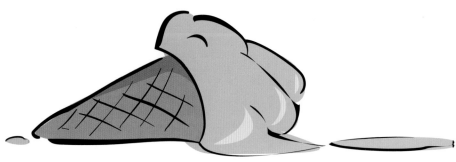

On an Ice Cream Run

Quilt size: 54" x 68"
Finished block size: 12" x 12"

ON AN ICE CREAM RUN, made by the author

It's 7:30 in the evening. Your favorite show is coming on TV at 8:00. You go to the freezer and… no ice cream! Does this ever happen to you? Who is the person in your family who goes on an ice cream "run?" Around here, whoever goes gets to choose the flavor.

Yardage and Cutting

Use fabric at least 40" wide. Cut strips selvage to selvage.

Fabric	Yards	First Cut	Second Cut
Block 1			
6 different colorways of coordinating light and dark prints	⅛ each light	1 strip 2 ½", each fabric	6 A ▢ 2 ½" x 2 ½" and 2 B ▭ 2 ½" x 4 ½", each fabric
	⅛ each dark	1 strip 2 ½", each fabric	6 A ▢ 2 ½" x 2 ½" and 2 B ▭ 2 ½" x 4 ½", each fabric
Light background	⅜	3 strips 2 ½"	48 A ▢ 2 ½" x 2 ½"
Gold	⅝	7 strips 2 ½"	24 B ▭ 2 ½" x 4 ½" 24 C ▭ 2 ½" x 6 ½"
Block 2			
Red	⅜	1 strip 2 ½"	(for strip piecing)
		2 strips 2 ½"	27 A ▢ 2 ½" x 2 ½"
Blue	⅜	1 strip 2 ½"	(for strip piecing)
		2 strips 2 ½"	27 A ▢ 2 ½" x 2 ½"
Light background	⅝	7 strips 2 ½"	24 B ▭ 2 ½" x 4 ½" 24 D ▭ 2 ½" x 8 ½"
Purple	1	6 strips 2 ½"	17 E ▭ 2 ½" x 12 ½" (sashing)
		6 strips 2 ½"	(inner border)
Outer border	1 ¼	7 strips 5 ½"	
Backing	4 ½	2 panels 32" x 76"	
Binding	⅝	7 strips 2 ½"	
Batting		62" x 76"	

Block Construction
Block 1

Each of the six blocks is made in a different colorway. The following instructions are for making one of these blocks.

1. Following the Corner-Square Flying Geese instructions on page 8, make two light and two dark Flying Geese units with coordinating light and dark B rectangles and eight light background A squares (fig. 1).

2. Make two two-patch units with A squares of the same light and dark prints (fig. 2).

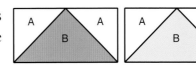

Fig. 1. Flying Geese units

3. Following the half-Flying Geese instructions on page 9, make two light and two dark half-Flying Geese units with A squares of the same light and dark fabrics and gold B rectangles (fig. 3). Make sure the direction of your diagonal seams matches the figure.

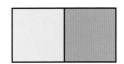

Make 2 in each colorway

Fig. 2. Two-patch unit

4. Assemble block 1 with the units from steps 1-3 and the C gold rectangles (fig. 4). Repeat in the other colorways for a total of six block 1.

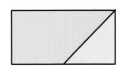

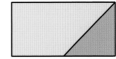

Fig. 3. Half-Flying Geese units

Block 2

1. Make a strip-set with the red and blue 2½" strips. Cut the strip-set into 12 segments 2½" (fig. 5, page 42).

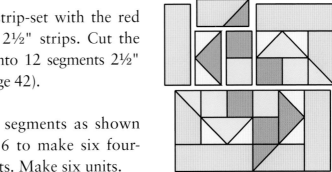

2. Join two segments as shown in figure 6 to make six four-patch units. Make six units.

Make 6

Fig. 4. Block-1 assembly

2½"

Fig. 5. Strip-set

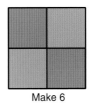

Make 6

Fig. 6. Four-patch unit

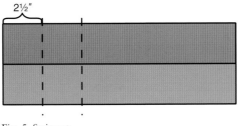

3. Referring to figure 7, make 24 block-2 rectangle units.

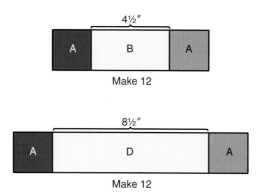

Make 12

Make 12

Fig. 7. Block-2 rectangle units

4. Follow the block assembly diagram to complete the block (fig. 8). Make six of block 2.

Quilt Assembly

1. Referring to the quilt assembly diagram (fig. 9), arrange the blocks, sashing strips, and six remaining A squares into rows. Sew the pieces together in rows then sew the rows together.

2. Square up the top and, measuring through the center of the quilt as described in Borders on page 10, cut and apply the inner and outer borders.

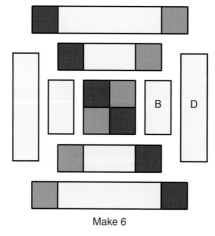

Make 6

Fig. 8. Block-2 assembly

Finishing

Layer the quilt top, batting, and backing; baste. Quilt the layers together then bind the raw edges to complete your quilt.

Design idea: To add some fun to this quilt, I decided to apply fusible web to the wrong side of some of the border fabric. I chose large flowers of different sizes and fused them across the center of the quilt, eliminating the middle sashing strip. The flowers were stitched around all the edges with invisible thread.

Fig. 9. Quilt assembly

Fortune Cookie Topping

Quilt size: 48" x 66½"
Finished block size: 12" x 12"

FORTUNE COOKIE TOPPING, made by the author

Use an Oriental-style fabric for the border. Once your quilt is finished, it's time to show it off. The next time you're having Chinese food with your friends, invite them home for dessert. Hang your new quilt for them to enjoy and dish up bowls of ice cream topped with fortune cookies.

Yardage and Cutting

Use fabric at least 40" wide. Cut strips selvage to selvage.

Fabric	Yards	First Cut	Second Cut
Green	⅝	1 strip 4 ½"	6 A ☐ 4 ½" x 4 ½"
		1 strip 5 ¼"	2 ⊠ 5 ¼" x 5 ¼"
			(total 8 B triangles)
		2 strips 2 ½"	(for strip piecing)
Red	½	1 strip 4 ½"	2 A ☐ 4 ½" x 4 ½"
		1 strip 5 ¼"	6 ⊠ 5 ¼" x 5 ¼"
			(total 24 B triangles)
		1 strip 2 ½"	(for strip piecing)
Orange	⅝	3 strips 5 ¼"	16 ⊠ 5 ¼" x 5 ¼" (total 64 B triangles)
		1 strip 1 ½"	17 C ☐ 1 ½" x 1 ½"
Black tone-on-tone	1 ⅞	1 strip 19 ⅝"	2 ⊠ 19 ⅝" x 19 ⅝"
			(total 6 G setting triangles, plus 2 extra)
		2 strips 5 ¼"	8 ⊠ 5 ¼" x 5 ¼" (total 32 B triangles)
		2 strips 4 ½"	32 D ▭ 2 ½" x 4 ½"
		3 strips 2 ½"	(strip piecing),
		8 strips 1 ½"	24 E ▭ 1 ½" x 12 ½"
Border print	1 ⅝	1 strip 10 ¾"	2 ◺ 10 ¾" x 10 ¾"
			(total 4 H corner setting triangles)
		7 strips 5 ½"	(outer border)
Backing	3 ¼	2 panels 37" x 56"	(horizontal quilt back seams)
Binding	⅝	7 strips 2 ½"	
Batting		55" x 74"	

Block Construction

1. Make two strip-sets with the black and green 2½" strips. Cut the strip-sets into 24 segments 2½" (fig. 1). Make one strip-set with the black and red 2½" strips. Cut this strip-set into 8 segments 2½".

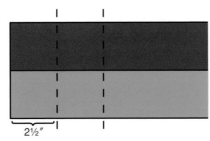

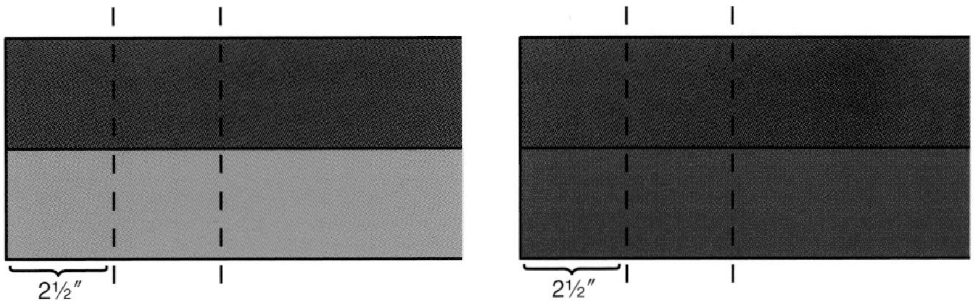

Fig. 1. Strip-sets for 2½" segments

2. Join each segment to a D rectangle to make the block corner units (fig. 2).

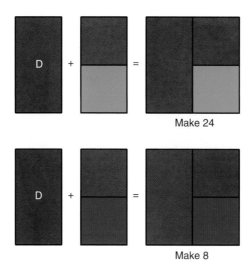

Make 24

Make 8

Fig. 2 Corner unit assembly

3. Make the quarter-square units with the B triangles (fig. 3).

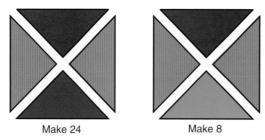

Make 24   Make 8

Fig. 3. Quarter-square unit assembly

4. Assemble the blocks (fig. 4).

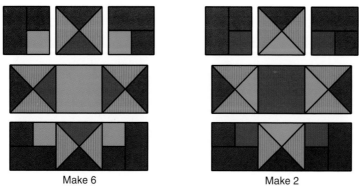

Make 6   Make 2

Fig. 4. Block assembly

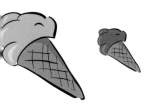

Quilt Assembly

1. With the orange D squares and the black E rectangles, make five sashing strips (fig. 5).

Make 2

Make 1

Make 2

Fig. 5. Sashing strips

2. Join the blocks and rows (fig. 6).

3. Measuring through the center as described in Borders on page 10, measure, cut, and add the borders to the quilt top.

Finishing

Layer the quilt top, batting, and backing; baste. Quilt the layers together, then bind the raw edges to complete your quilt.

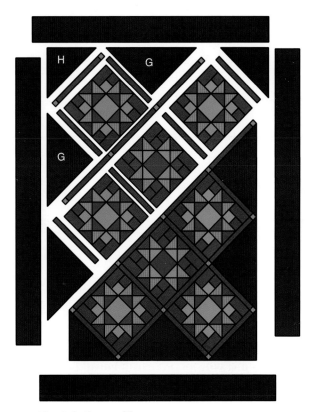

Fig. 6. Quilt assembly

Chocolate Ripple

Quilt size: 51" x 63"
Finished block size: 6" x 6"

CHOCOLATE RIPPLE, made by the author

Chocolate. Just saying the word makes most of us smile. If I were to have ice cream just the way I wanted, it would be chocolate, of course. But it would have a few things added, like marshmallows, toasted almonds, crumbles of Heath candy bars, and white chocolate covered nuts. Of course, it would have to have toppings: caramel, hot fudge, and whipped cream. Yum! That was the inspiration for this quilt.

This is a great stash quilt. The scrappier it is, the better.

Yardage and Cutting

Use fabric at least 40" wide. Cut strips selvage to selvage.

Fabric	Yards	First Cut	Second Cut
Light background	½	2 strips 2 ½"	18 A ☐ 2 ½" x 2 ½"
		3 strips 2 ⅞"	36 B ☐ 2 ⅞" x 2 ⅞"
Brown tone-on-tone	⅜	3 strips 2 ⅞"	36 B ☐ 2 ⅞" x 2 ⅞"
Rust	⅜	5 strips 1 ½"	(for strip piecing C segments)
Gold	⅜	5 strips 1 ½"	(for strip piecing C segments)
Paisley	1 ⅛	2 strips 2 ⅝"	17 D ☐ 2 ⅝" x 2 ⅝"
		2 strips 4 ¼"	17 E ⊠ 4 ¼" x 4 ¼"
		3 strips 2 ⅜"	34 F ◩ 2 ⅜" x 2 ⅜"
		1 strip 8"	4 H ☐ 8" x 8"
Assorted medium prints	1 ½ total	5 strips 2 ⅝"	68 D ☐ 2 ⅝" x 2 ⅝"
		4 strips 8 ⅞"	14 G ☐ 8 ⅞" x 8 ⅞"
Light border background	1 ⅛	4 strips 8 ⅞"	14 G ☐ 8 ⅞" x 8 ⅞"
Inner border 1	⅜	4 strips 2"	
Inner border 2	⅜	5 strips 2"	
Backing	3 ½	2 panels 37" x 59"	
Binding	⅜	7 strips 2 ½"	
Batting		59" x 71"	

You can use a mix of fat quarters for this quilt. You will need twice as many strips as the cutting instructions indicate.

Block Construction

1. Following the Half-Square Triangle instructions on page 8, make 72 half-square triangle units with the 36 light background and 36 brown tone-on-tone B squares.

2. Make five strip-sets with the rust and gold 1½" strips. Cut 72 segments 2½" (fig. 1).

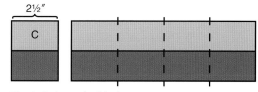

2½"

C

Fig. 1. Strip-set for block-1 segments

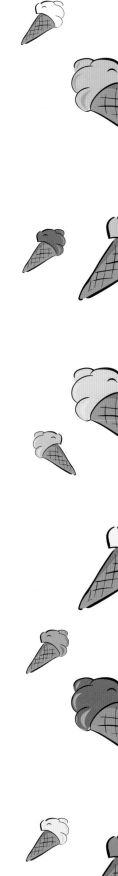

3. Assemble block 1 (fig. 2). Make 18.

4. Referring to figure 3, assemble block 2. Make 17.

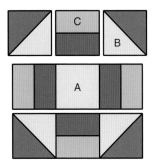

Fig. 2. Block-1 assembly

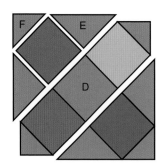

Fig. 3. Block-2 assembly

Quilt Assembly

1. Lay out the quilt top in seven rows of five blocks, alternating the placement of blocks 1 and 2. See the quilt assembly, page 51.

2. Join the rows. Square up the quilt top before adding the borders and, measuring through the center as described in Borders on page 10, add the first and second inner borders. The quilt should measure 36½" x 48½", including seam allowances.

3. Make 28 half-square triangles with the 14 G light border background squares and 14 assorted G squares. Divide the units into two piles of 14 each. Turn the piles so that the diagonal on one pile slants up and the diagonal on the other pile slants down (fig. 4).

Fig. 4. Border half-square triangles

4. Cut each half-square triangle into 2" segments. Rearrange the segments as shown in figures 5 and 6 using four segments from four different half-square triangles to create a scrappy look. Join the segments to make 28 border units.

Quilts for Ice Cream Lovers ∴ Janet Jones Worley

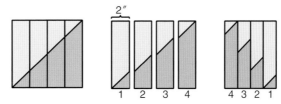

Fig. 5. Up-slant segments create a down-slant border unit.

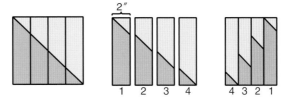

Fig. 6. Down-slant segments create an up-slant border unit.

5. Join eight border units as shown in figure 7 to form the side borders and add to the quilt. Join six border units plus two H squares at each end to form the top and bottom borders and add to the quilt.

Finishing

Layer the quilt top, batting, and backing; baste. Quilt the layers together then bind the raw edges to complete your quilt.

Fig. 7. Quilt assembly

Girlie Girl Grape

Quilt size: 41½" x 54"
Finished block size: 9" x 9"

GIRLIE GIRL GRAPE, made by the author

Once upon a road trip, my friend Kimma decided we must have some Brewster's grape ice cream in honor of my new book. Having never heard of such a thing, I was game. We went to a wonderful ice cream shop near Atlanta, Georgia. Kimma was crushed to find they had no grape ice cream and shocked to be told that they had never had any. To this day, she swears she had the most wonderful grape ice cream there, and no one can tell her any different.

Kimma, this quilt's for you. May everyone have a friend who drags them off to an ice cream shop.

Yardage and Cutting

Use fabric at least 40" wide. Cut strips selvage to selvage, unless noted otherwise.

Fabric	Yards	First Cut	Second Cut
Large print	1 ¾	1 strip 9 ½"	2 B ☐ 9 ½" x 9 ½"
border 4		2 strips 5 ½" x 47"	(cut parallel to selvages)
		2 strips 5 ½" x 44"	
Deep purple	¾	1 strip 3 ½"	3 A ☐ 3 ½" x 3 ½"
		2 strips 1 ½"	(strip piecing)
borders 1 & 3		9 strips 1 ½"	
Lavender	½	8 strips 1 ½"	(strip piecing)
Purple print	¼	3 strips 1 ½"	(strip piecing)
Light green	¼	3 strips 1 ½"	(strip piecing)
Dark peach	¼	1 strip 3 ½"	3 A ☐ 3 ½" x 3 ½"
		2 strips 1 ½"	(strip piecing)
Light peach	¼	3 strips 1 ½"	(strip piecing)
Medium green	¼	3 strips 1 ½"	(strip piecing)
Lavender print	¾	1 strip 14"	2 ⊠ 14" x 14"
			(total 6 C, plus 2 extra)
		1 strip 7 ¼"	2 ◺ 7 ¼" x 7 ¼"
			(total 4 D)
Backing	3	2 panels 32" x 50"	
Binding	⅝	6 strips 2 ½"	
Batting		50" x 62"	

Block Construction

1. Make one strip-set with two lavender and one deep purple 1½" strips. Cut into 24 segments 1½" (fig. 1, page 54).

2. Make two strip-sets with one each light green, lavender, and purple print 1½" strips as shown in figure 1. Cut into 12 segments 1½" and 12 segments 3½". Press the seam allowances toward the darker fabric.

3. Make 12 nine-patch units with three 1½" segments as shown in figure 1.

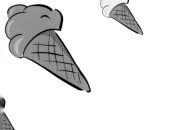

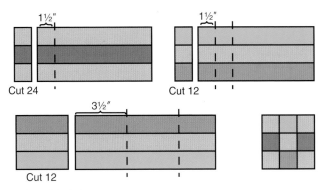

Fig. 1. Block 1 segments

4. Make three block 1 with the nine-patch units, the 3½" segments, and the deep purple A squares.

5. Make one strip-set with two lavender and one dark peach 1½" strips. Cut into 24 segments 1½".

6. Make two strip-sets with one each light peach, lavender, and medium green 1½" strips as shown in figure 3. Cut into 12 segments 1½" and 12 segments 3½". Press the seam allowances toward the darker fabric (fig. 3).

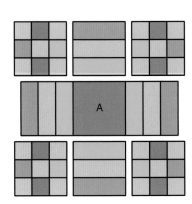

Fig. 2. Block 1 assembly

7. Make 12 nine-patch units with three 1½" segments (fig. 3).

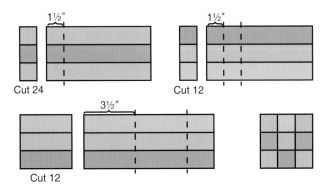

Fig. 3. Block 2 segments

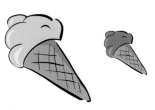

8. Make three block 2 with the nine-patch units, the 3½" segments, and the dark peach A squares (fig. 4).

Quilt Assembly

1. Join the pieced blocks, the B squares, and the C and D triangles in diagonal rows, then join those rows (fig. 5).

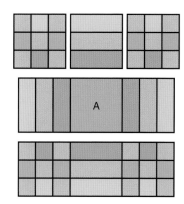

Fig. 4. Block-2 assembly

2. Square up the top and, measuring through the center of the quilt as described in Borders on page 10, measure, cut, and apply the border-1 strips. Press the seam allowances toward the border.

3. For pieced border-2, make a strip-set with six 1½" strips, one of each block fabric, arranged in any order (fig. 6). Press all the seam allowances in the same direction. Cut the strip-set into twenty-four 1½" segments.

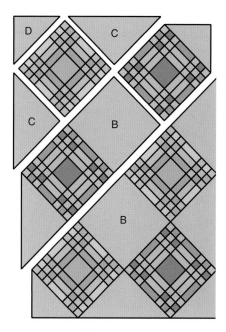

Fig. 5. Assembling the blocks

4. Measure the length of your quilt as before. Join six segments end to end and add as much of a seventh segment as needed to form a pieced border equal to the quilt's length. Make two of these. If your pieced border strip doesn't quite fit, adjust several of the segment seam allowances to get the measurement you need.

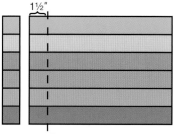

Fig. 6. Border-2 strip-set

5. Sew the pieced border strips to the sides of the quilt top. Press the seam allowances toward border 1.

6. In the same manner, measure and sew five segments end to end and add as much of a sixth segment, if needed, to make a pieced border equal to the quilt's width. Make two of these. Sew these strips to the top and bottom of the quilt.

7. Measuring as before, add borders 3 and 4 to the quilt. Press the seam allowances toward the outer border (fig. 7).

Finishing

Layer the quilt top, batting, and backing; baste. Quilt the layers together, then bind the raw edges to complete your quilt.

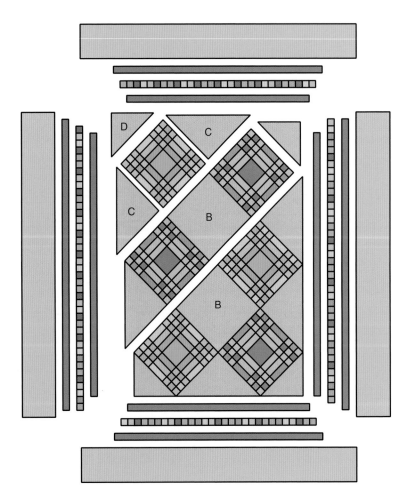

Fig. 7. Completed quilt top

Cherry on Top

CHERRY ON TOP, made by the author

This quilt is done by chain piecing all the blocks at once. It is fast, fun, and simple to do. You are going to love it because you can just sit and sew until it's time for an ice cream break!

Yardage and Cutting

Use fabric at least 40" wide. Cut strips selvage to selvage.

Fabric	Yards	Cut
Assorted light fabrics	3 ⅛ total	1 ½" strips
Assorted dark fabrics	3 ⅝ total	1 ½" strips
Red	2 ⅛	3 strips 2 ½" cut into 48 squares 2 ½" x 2 ½" (centers)
outer border		9 strips 6 ½"
inner border	⅝	8 strips 2"
Backing	6	2 panels 40" x 103"
Binding	⅞	10 strips 2 ½"
Batting	83" x 103"	

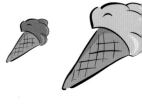
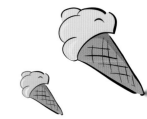

Using an assembly-line method helps speed up making the blocks. One important detail—as each unit is sewn to a strip, gently press the seam allowances toward the strip before cutting the units apart.

Block Construction

1. Sew the red center squares to a light strip, leaving a small space between the squares (fig. 1). Press the seam allowances toward the strips. Cut the units apart, making sure the cut is straight. You want to always keep your block square.

2. Rotate the units 90 degrees and sew them to a second light strip (fig. 2). Press, then cut the units apart as before.

3. Rotate the units 90 degrees and sew them to the first dark strip. Press, then cut the units apart (fig. 3).

4. Add the second dark strip, and continue adding two light strips, then two dark strips, until the blocks have eight light and eight dark strips, ending with a second dark strip (fig. 4). The blocks should measure 10½" x 10½".

Quilt Assembly

1. Arrange the blocks in eight rows of six blocks to match the quilt or play around with the placement until you find a layout you like. Join the blocks.

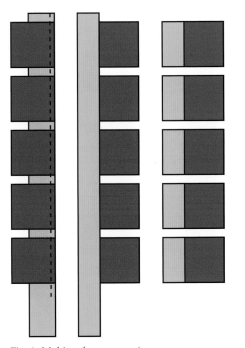

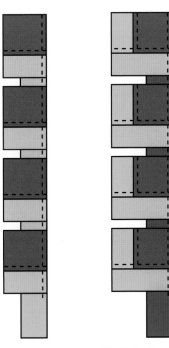

Fig. 1. Making the center units

Fig. 2. Adding the second light strip

Fig. 3. Adding the first dark strip

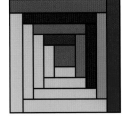

Fig. 4. Completed block

2. Measuring through the center as described in Borders on page 10, measure, cut, and add the inner and outer borders to the quilt top.

Finishing

Layer the quilt top, batting, and backing; baste. Quilt the layers together, then bind the raw edges to complete your quilt.

Quilt assembly

Cherry on Top Mantel Scarf

Quilt size: 23" x 57"
Finished block size: 10" x 10"

CHERRY ON TOP MANTEL SCARF, made by the author

This is a great, fast project that requires no binding. Don't worry if you do not have a fireplace with a mantel. I've made five of these and I don't have a mantel either. These can go on the edge of a counter, a long table, or across the back of a couch. Use your imagination. They make great gifts.

Yardage and Cutting

Use fabric at least 40" wide. Cut strips selvage to selvage, unless noted otherwise.

Fabric	Yards	Cut
Assorted light fabrics	½ total	1 ½" strips
Assorted dark fabrics	½ total	1 ½" strips
Red centers	⅛	3 ☐ 2 ½" x 2 ½"
Remaining pieces		
3 side triangles	2 ¼	1 ⊠ 15 ½" x 15 ½"
2 corner triangles		1 ◹ 8" x 8"
mantel section		1 rectangle 9 ½" x 59" cut parallel to the selvage
Backing		1 piece 26" x 59"
Batting		26" x 59"

Quilts for Ice Cream Lovers ⦂ Janet Jones Worley

Mantel Scarf Construction

1. Make four Log Cabin blocks according to Block Construction steps 1–4 on page 58.

2. Join the blocks with three side triangles and two corner triangles, then add the mantel section as shown in figure 1.

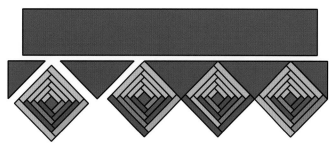

Fig. 1. Mantel scarf assembly

3. Layer the mantel scarf and backing, right sides together, then add the batting. Baste together by hand or with #1 quilting safety pins.

4. Stitch around the edges, leaving a 10" opening on the long straight edge for turning.

5. Trim the points, clip the Vs between the blocks, remove the basting pins, and turn the mantel scarf right side out.

6. Push out the points with the tool of your choice. I love to use a wooden chopstick.

7. Stitch the opening closed by hand. Press and sew around the mantel scarf ¼" from the edge to create a faux binding. Baste again and quilt as desired.

Quilting Suggestion

To keep this project as simple and fast as possible, keep the quilting to a minimum. Using a walking foot, stitch from the point of each block and setting triangle, straight across to the outer edge of the mantel section. Stitch in the ditch along the seam joining the mantel section to the blocks and stitch around the scarf ¼" from the edge to give the illusion of a binding.

Blueberry Sauce

Quilt size: 36" x 36"
Finished appliqué block size: 14" x 14"
Finished pieced block size: 6" x 6"

BLUEBERRY SAUCE, made by the author

One year, I went blueberry picking on the Illinois-Indiana border. I had no idea blueberries could grow that big! They were so large we could not make muffins with them unless we cut them in quarters. Oh, they were wonderful.

Another piece of heaven is fresh blueberry sauce on ice cream or, better yet, on cheesecake. Anyone who wants some company blueberry picking, just give me a call. Those wonderful berries were the inspiration for this quilt.

Yardage and Cutting

Use fabric at least 40" wide. Cut strips selvage to selvage.

Fabric	Yards	First Cut	Second Cut
Light blue	⅝	2 strips 2"	12 H ▭ 2" x 3 ½"
		4 strips 2"	64 I ▢ 2" x 2"
		1 strip 3 ½"	8 J ▢ 3 ½" x 3 ½"
		appliqué pieces	
Dark blue	1	4 strips 2"	64 I ▢ 2" x 2"
		1 strip 3 ½"	8 J ▢ 3 ½" x 3 ½"
border 1		2 strips 1"	
border 2		4 strips 3 ½"	
		appliqué pieces	
White	1 ⅜	12 strips 2"	72 H ▭ 2" x 3 ½"
			92 I ▢ 2" x 2"
		1 strip 16½"	1 G ▢ 16 ½" x 16 ½"
Backing	1 ¼	1 panel 40" x 40"	
Binding	⅜	4 strips 2 ½"	
Batting		40" x 40"	

Appliqué Block Construction

1. Make the appliqué pieces using the templates on page 65.

2. Fold the white G square in quarters diagonally and gently finger press to establish placement lines.

3. Arrange the pieces as shown in figure 1 on page 64, and fuse them in place in alphabetical order. Finish the raw edges with a small zigzag stitch in monofilament or matching thread.

Eight-Pointed Star Block Construction

1. Make 32 Flying Geese units with white H rectangles and light blue I squares. Make 32 more units with white H rectangles and dark blue I squares.

Fig. 1. Appliqué block assembly

2. Make eight light blue and eight dark blue Eight-Pointed Star blocks as shown in figure 2.

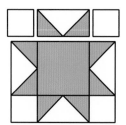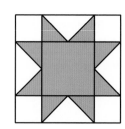

Fig. 2. Eight-Pointed Star block assembly

Quilt Assembly

1. Trim the appliqué block to 14½" x 14½". Measure through the center as described in Borders on page 10. Cut the 1" dark blue border strips to size and add them to the center appliqué block.

2. For the inner pieced border, make 12 Flying Geese units with the light blue H rectangles and white I squares.

3. Make four border strips with 12 Flying Geese units, four white I squares, and eight white H rectangles (fig. 3). Add the border units to the quilt.

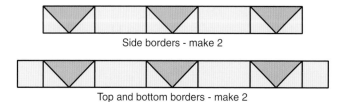

Side borders - make 2

Top and bottom borders - make 2

Fig. 3. Pieced border assembly

4. Add the Eight-Pointed Star blocks, alternating the light and blue blocks as shown in figure 4.

5. Measure, cut, and apply the outer border.

Finishing

Layer the quilt top, batting, and backing; baste. Quilt the layers together, then bind the raw edges to complete your quilt.

Fig. 4. Quilt assembly

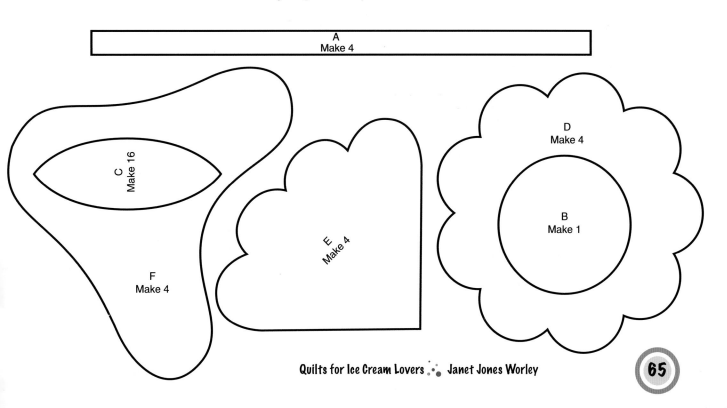

Red Velvet Ice Cream

Quilt size: 48" x 58"
Finished block size: 12" x 12"

RED VELVET ICE CREAM, made by the author

Red velvet cake! The second best dessert on the planet. You may ask, "What is the first?" A birthday cake from Peggy Ann's Bakery in Huntsville, Alabama.

My wonderful friend Pam Lapier makes a red velvet cake that is amazing. During the holidays, she and Kimma (my grape ice cream friend) came over for a cooking lesson and taught me how to make Pam's cake and Kimma's best-ever dressing. Right then, I decided I had to design a quilt in honor of this cake that I can now make from scratch. Serve it with vanilla ice cream. Better yet, mush the cake into the ice cream and refreeze. Voila! Red velvet ice cream.

Yardage and Cutting

Use fabric at least 40" wide. Cut strips selvage to selvage, unless noted otherwise.

Fabric	Yards	Cut
Dark red #1	1 ½	6 strips 2 ½"
		16E, 16 Er
border 1		2 strips 2" x 38 ½"
		2 strips 3 ½" x 41 ½"
		cut parallel to selvages
Dark red #2	½	36 A
Assorted reds	1 total or 4 fat quarters	1 strip 4"
		12 half-strips, 2 ½" x 20"
		3 strips 1 ½" cut into 7 ☐ 1 ½" x 12"
		64 B, 2 C
White	2 ¾	
border 2		2 strips 6 ½" x 46 ½"
		2 strips 10" x 52 ½" cut parallel to selvages
		5 ☐ 13" x 13"
		6 half-strips 2 ½" x 20"
		16 D
Backing		2 panels 28" x 66"
Batting		56" x 66"

Additional Supplies

fabric marker that will show on red
1 package or 1 yard fusible web
⅛" bias bar
Water-soluble thread
Template plastic
Beads

Appliqué Block Construction

1. See The Scoop on Fusing on page 9. Make 36 appliqué A pieces of dark red #2 (16 of the pieces will be for the outer border appliqué).

2. Make 64 appliqué B pieces of the assorted reds (24 of the pieces will be for the outer border appliqué).

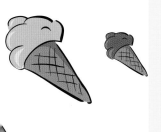

3. For the stems, cut 20 strips 1" wide on the bias from the 4" wide strip of red. Fold each strip lengthwise, wrong sides together, and sew with a ⅛" seam allowance, to make a tube. Trim the seam allowances to a scant ⅛".

4. Insert a ⅛" bias bar into the tube and press, folding the seam allowances to the back. Trim each stem to 5".

 The Scoop: Alternate Bias Tube Method

If you have shied away from making bias tubes, give this method a try:

Fold a square of fabric (fig. a) on the diagonal, wrong sides together, forming a triangle (fig. b). Sew a line of stitching parallel to the folded edge the width of your finished bias tube (fig. c).

Sew about 5", pause with the needle in the down position, insert a bias bar into the tube to make sure it fits, then stitch to the end of the tube.

Cut off the tube (fig. d), leaving a scant ⅛" seam allowance.

Insert a ⅛" bias bar and press, folding the seam allowances to the back (fig. e). Carefully remove the bar. (If it's metal, it's hot.) Let the fabric cool. Then press again to get the tube as flat as possible. Cut off the length you need.

You can then fold over the edge of a remaining triangle about 1", wrong sides together, and sew another tube (fig. f).

wrong side

Fig a.

right side

fold

Fig b.

right

Fig c.

right

Fig d.

press

Fig e.

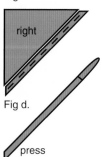

wrong

fold

Fig f.

5. Fold a 13" x 13" white square in quarters diagonally and carefully finger press to establish placement lines. Arrange and fuse four A pieces along the fold lines, starting 2" from the center of the block (fig. 1). Arrange and fuse eight B pieces.

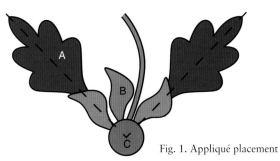

Fig. 1. Appliqué placement

6. Baste four stems in place with a line of stitching down the middle in water-soluble thread. Use monofilament or matching thread to finish the edges with a small zigzag stitch.

7. Finish the center of the appliqué with ruching (see The Scoop on Ruching). Trim the block to 12½" x 12½". Repeat to make a total of five appliqué blocks.

 The Scoop on Ruching

1. Trace the zigzag line onto template plastic or cardboard and cut the template.

2. For the ruched centers, fold in the long edges of the seven 1½" strips in so they meet in the center, wrong sides together. Press. Use the template (page 73) to draw a zigzag guideline on the front of the strip, making sure the points touch the edges of the strip.

3. With needle and thread, make a running stitch along the zigzag line, taking an extra stitch at the top of each point, looping the thread over the edge of the strip and bringing the needle from the back to front. Pull up the thread to gather the strip every few inches and take an extra stitch over a running stitch to secure the gathers.

4. Place the ruched circle in the center of the appliqué block, tuck under the ends, and stitch in place.

Star Block Construction

1. Make six strip-sets with the white and assorted red 2½" half-strips. Cut a total of 32 segments 2½". Join two segments from different strip-sets to make 16 four-patch corner units (fig. 2).

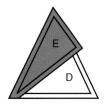

Fig. 2. Four-patch corner unit

2. Make three strip-sets with the six remaining assorted red half-strips. Cut a total of eight segments 2½", and join two segments from different strip-sets to make four all red center four-patch units.

3. Trace templates D and E onto template plastic and cut on the traced line. Trace and cut 16 D from white fabric, and 16 E and 16 E-reverse from dark red #1. Join the D and E pieces to form a star point unit. Make 16.

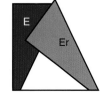

Fig. 3. Star-point unit

4. Referring to figure 4, make four Star blocks.

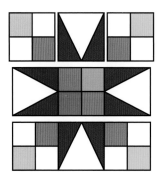

Fig. 4 Star-block assembly

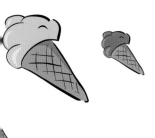

The Scoop: Alternate Star-Point Method

A template has been provided to paper piece the star-point unit, if you prefer. Make 16 copies. The yardage requirements provide enough fabric for either method.

1. Cut 16 dark red #2 rectangles 3½" x 6". Cut eight rectangles in half on the diagonal (E) and cut eight on the opposite diagonal (Er).

2. Cut 16 white 3¾" x 3¾" squares.

3. Paper piece 16 star-point units, remove the paper, and trim the units to 3½" x 3½".

Quilt Assembly

1. Arrange the appliqué and Star blocks as shown in the quilt assembly on page 72 and join the rows.

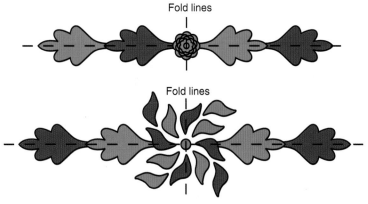

Fig. 5. Outer border appliqué placement

2. Measuring through the center as described in Borders on page 10, add the side inner borders (2" strips) and the top and bottom inner borders (3½" strips) of dark red-1.

The outer borders are cut extra wide and long to allow for take-up during the appliqué process. The side borders will finish 4½" wide, and the top and bottom borders 8" wide.

3. Fold the outer border strips in quarters and finger press to create placement lines as shown in figure 5, on page 71.

4. Place and fuse the appliqué pieces. Finish the appliqué edges with a narrow zigzag stitch. Fasten a ruched piece in the center of each side border.

5. Trim the side borders to 8½" wide and the top and bottom borders to 5" wide.

6. Measure your quilt and cut the side borders to the correct size and add them to the quilt top.

7. Measure your quilt and cut the top and bottom borders to the correct size and add them to the quilt top.

Finishing

Layer the quilt top, batting, and backing; baste. Quilt the layers together, then bind the raw edges to complete your quilt. Embellish the appliquéd stems with beads.

Fig. 6. Quilt assembly

A

C

B

E/Er

D

Snip and Toss Cone Caddy

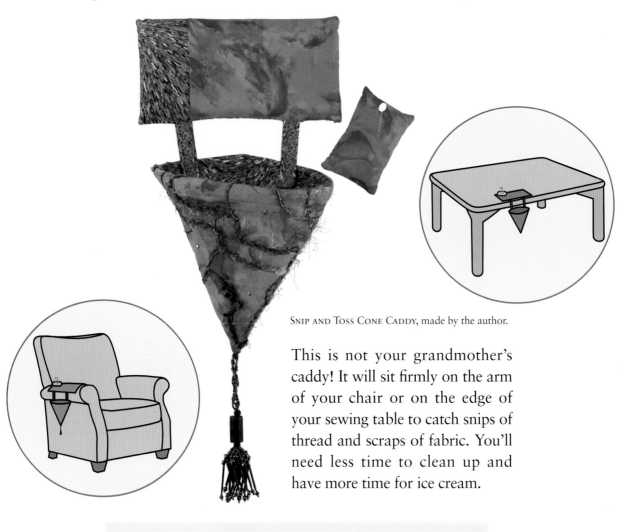

SNIP AND TOSS CONE CADDY, made by the author.

This is not your grandmother's caddy! It will sit firmly on the arm of your chair or on the edge of your sewing table to catch snips of thread and scraps of fabric. You'll need less time to clean up and have more time for ice cream.

Materials

3 fat quarters
Two ¼" thick rectangular tiles 3" x 8"
Strip of batting approximately 9" x 15"
18" square of freezer paper
½ yard fusible interfacing or tear-away stabilizer
1 yard or 1 package of boning
6" Velcro®
1 bead tassel 2 ½" to 3" long
Beads and trims for embellishment
Polyfil stuffing for the pincushion

 *The Scoop* You'll need to stack two ¼" thick tiles for enough weight to hold the caddy in place. I found a ½" thick tile that was heavy enough by itself.

Directions are written for tiles 3" x 8". You'll need to cut your fabric rectangles larger or smaller, depending on the size of the tiles you use.

Making the Cone

1. Cut an 18" circle from the freezer paper. Fold the circle in half and cut it on the fold. Fold the half circle in half three times, accordion style, to eliminate bulk. Unfold and cut off two of the wedges to form your cone template (fig. 1).

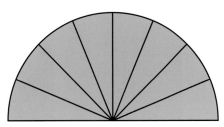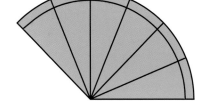

Fig. 1 Making the cone template

 *Making a Circle*
To make an 18" circle, fold an 18" square of freezer paper in quarters. Thread a needle and knot the end. Open the folded paper and come up from the shiny side through the center point with your needle and thread. Measure 9" from the center and use the thread to guide a pencil to mark a circle on the paper.

2. Trace the cone template on the back of two fat quarters (one for the outside and one for the lining) and on the stabilizer. Cut out the three pieces. Fuse the stabilizer to the back of the fabric you want for the outside of your caddy.

3. Using decorative stitches, free-motion couching, trims, ribbons, etc., turn your cone into a work of art. Be careful not to place any beads or charms within ¼" of the side edges or within 1" of the curved edge. You can add bulky embellishments after you've assembled the cone.

4. With right sides together, sew the embellished and lining fabrics together and stitch around all the edges, leaving a 3" opening on both sides (fig. 2). Clip the curves and turn the piece right side out. Fold in the ¼" seam allowances on both openings to the inside and press.

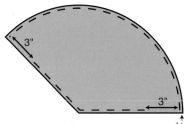

Fig. 2. Sewing the cone

5. Stitch the loop of your bead tassel to the inside point of the cone. Sew a line of stitching ¾" in from the curved edge, creating a channel (fig. 3). Insert a 20" piece of boning. Overlap and glue the ends. Stitch the remaining side openings closed by hand. Whipstitch the finished edges together to form the cone.

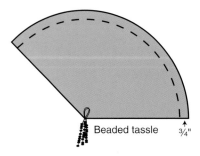

Beaded tassle   ¾"

Fig. 3. Adding the tassel and stitching the channel

Making the Caddy
1. From the remaining fabric, cut:
   2 rectangles 7" x 9½"
   1 rectangle 7" x 14"
   4 rectangles 1½" x 4"
   2 squares 4" x 4"

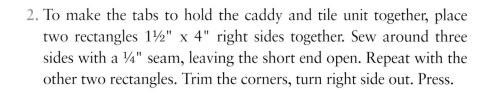

2. To make the tabs to hold the caddy and tile unit together, place two rectangles 1½" x 4" right sides together. Sew around three sides with a ¼" seam, leaving the short end open. Repeat with the other two rectangles. Trim the corners, turn right side out. Press.

3. Layer the three rectangles (fig. 4):
   • 7 x 9½" rectangle right side up with the tabs placed along the edge about 3½" apart
   • 7" x 14" rectangle, folded wrong sides together to make a 7" x 7" square, aligning raw edges with the first rectangle (to form a pocket in the top of the tile unit to hold scissors, ruler, etc.)
   • 7 x 9½" rectangle wrong side up

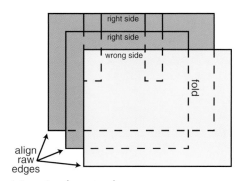

Fig. 4. Layering the rectangles

4. Sew around four sides of the layered rectangles with a ¼" seam allowance, leaving a 4½" opening along one end. Trim the corners and turn right side out.

5. Wrap the batting strip around the tiles twice (trimming the batting if necessary) and slide the tiles in through the open end. Close the seam by hand.

Finishing

1. Sew around the 4" x 4" squares, leaving a 2" opening on one side. Trim the corners and turn the square right side out. Stuff the square with polyfil and close the opening by hand. Sew or glue the square to the end of the tile unit.

2. Attach a strip of the loop half of Velcro fastening tape to the tabs on the tile unit. Attach the hook half to the cone.

About the Author

Janet Jones Worley is a professional teacher, quilter, designer, and author. She has a quilt on permanent display in the library of Beijing, China. Many of her designs have been published by *McCall's Quilting*, *McCall's Quick Quilts*, *Traditional Quilter*, *Quick and Easy Crafts*, and various House of White Birches publications. Janet has appeared on Alex Anderson's *Simply Quilts*, WHNT news, and on Canadian television.

Janet's Web site (www.JanetJonesWorley.com) has contact information, teaching schedules, quilts, patterns, and more. Although Janet loves designing, her first love is teaching. She travels and teaches as much as possible and loves every minute. To date she has taught in almost every state in the United States as well as in Canada and Europe. Her lighthearted approach to quilting makes her classes fun and exciting.

Many of Janet's quilts can be seen in national and international quilt shows and trade shows in the United States and Europe. Although most of her work is traditional, she is drawn to innovative techniques and styles. In her free time she makes one-of-kind art quilts purely for pleasure. At this time Janet has a quilt in the Alzheimer's Art Quilt Initiative and the Pilgrim/Roy Challenge.

Resources

The companies listed here provided fabrics and threads used in my quilts.

Superior Threads
PO Box 1672
St. George, UT 84771
Phone: 800-499-1777
Web site: www.superiorthreads.com
E-mail: info@superiorthreads.com

The Warm Company
5529 186th Place SW
Lynnwood, WA 98037
Phone: 425-248-2424
Web site: www.warmcompany.com
Makers of the Insul-Bright batting for potholders and hot pads

Hobbs Bonded Fibers – Batting
200 South Commerce Dr.
Waco, TX 76710
Phone: 800-443-3357
Web site: www.hobbsbondedfibers.com

In the Beginning Fabrics
Seattle, WA
Web site: www.inthebeginningfabrics.com

Bernina® of America, Inc.
3702 Prairie Lake Court
Aurora, IL 60504
Phone: 630-978-2500
Web site: www.berninausa.com

Debbie Bowles
Maple Island Quilts
329 Maple Island Road
Burnsville, MN 55306
Web site: www.mapleislandquilts.com
E-mail: info@mapleislandquilts.com

Bali Fabrics
21787 Eighth Street East Suite #1
Sonoma CA 95476
Web site: www.balifab.com

Benartex, Inc. – Fabrics
1359 Broadway, Suite 1100
New York, NY 10018
Info@benartex.com
Web site: www.benartex.com

Lucy Fazely Designs
PO Box 492
Oscoda, MI 48750
Website: www.lucyfazely.com
E-mail: lucy@lucyfazely.com

Robert Kaufman Co. – Fabrics
129 West 132nd St.
Los Angeles, CA 90061
Phone: 800-877-2066
Website: www.robertkaufman.com
Sells fabrics wholesale and to the trade.
Web site includes a store locator.

Michael Miller Fabrics, LLC
118 West 22nd Street, 5th Floor
New York, NY 10011
Web site: www.michaelmillerfabrics.com
E-mail: info@michaelmillerfabrics.com

Kreinik Manufacturing Company, Inc.
1708 Gihon Road
Parkersburg, WV
Phone: 800-537-2166
Web site: www.kreinik.com
E-mail: information@kreinik.com

Other AQS Books

This is only a small selection of the books available from the American Quilter's Society. AQS books are known worldwide for timely topics, clear writing, beautiful color photos, and accurate illustrations and patterns. The following books are available from your local bookseller, quilt shop, or public library.

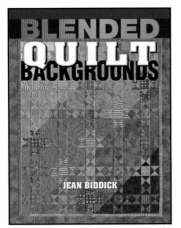

#7078   us$24.95

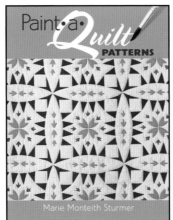

#7016   us$22.95

#6805   us$22.95

#7012   us$19.95

#7079   us$22.95

#7010   us$21.95

#7014   us$24.95

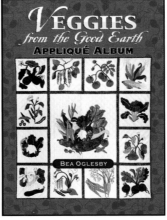

#7017   us$21.95

#6904   us$21.95

Look for these books nationally. 1-800-626-5420
Call or Visit our Web site at www.AmericanQuilter.com